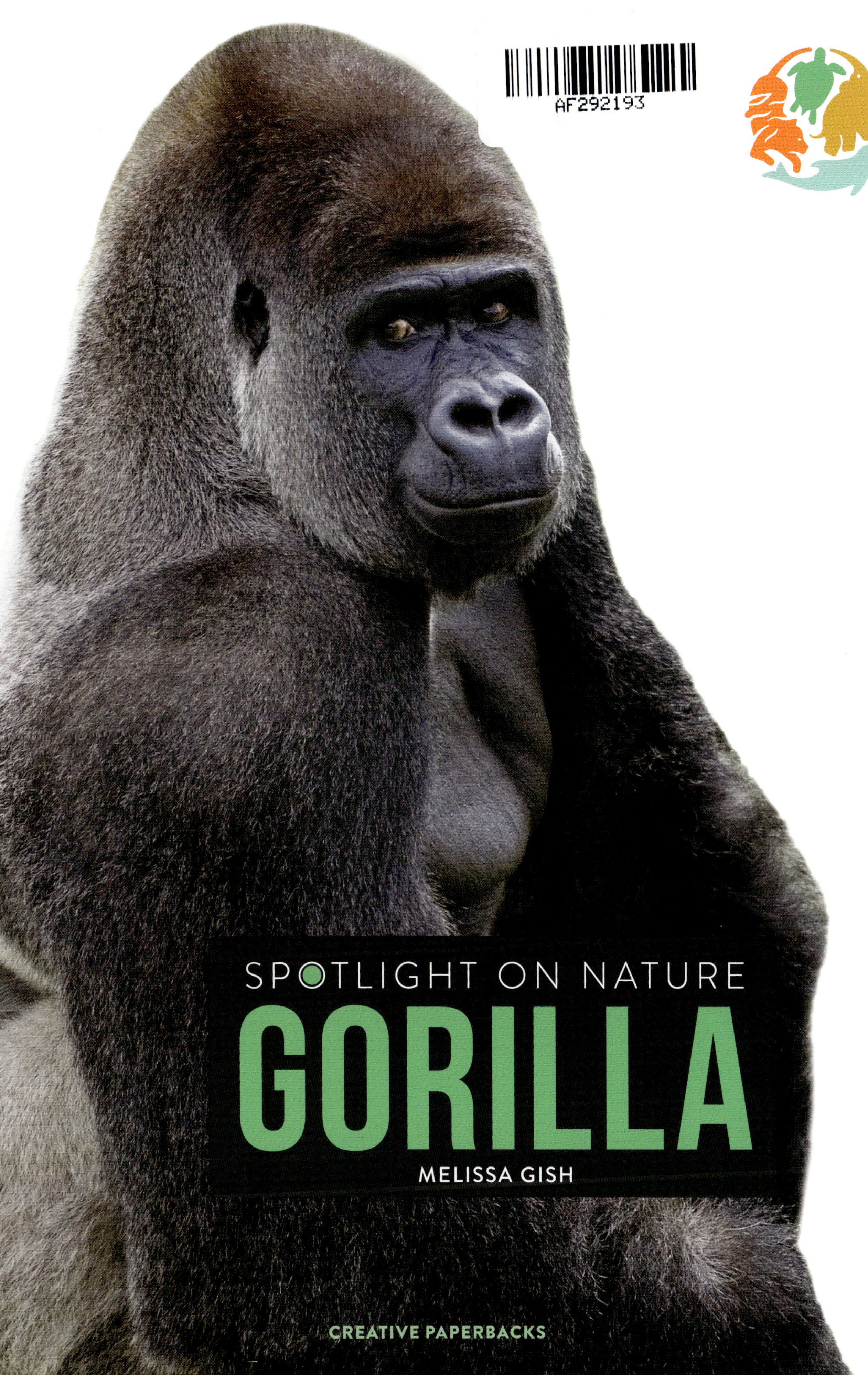
SPOTLIGHT ON NATURE
GORILLA
MELISSA GISH
CREATIVE PAPERBACKS

Published by Creative Paperbacks
P.O. Box 227, Mankato, Minnesota 56002
Creative Paperbacks is an imprint of
The Creative Company
www.thecreativecompany.us

Design by Chelsey Luther; production by Colin O'Dea
Art direction by Rita Marshall
Printed in the United States of America

Photographs by Alamy (AF archive, David Cantrille, Eric Gevaert, Nature Picture Library, Jamie Pham), Getty Images (Lisle Brathwaite/500px Prime, Ibrahim Suha Derbent/Photodisc, Education Images/Universal Images Group, Jupiterimages/liquidlibrary, Jacob Maentz/Corbis Documentary, Francis Miller/The LIFE Picture Collection, HENDRIK SCHMIDT/Stringer/ DPA), iStockphoto (ajball18, Alan_Lagadu, antpkr, aznature, guenterguni, Max_grpo, Lina Moiseienko, Cheryl Ramalho, Grant Thomas), Minden Pictures (Suzi Eszterhas, Jabruson/NPL), National Geographic Creative (CHRIS SCHMID), Shutterstock (LMIMAGES)

Library of Congress Cataloging-in-Publication Data
is available under PCN 2020901932.
ISBN 978-1-68277-033-7 (pbk)

First UK Edition 9 8 7 6 5 4 3 2 1

CONTENTS

MOUNTAIN GORILLAS

of Bwindi Impenetrable Forest

Bwindi Impenetrable Forest in southwestern Uganda is one of the most heavily forested places on the planet. On Bwindi's mountains, thick vines fill the spaces between soaring sapele mahogany and shorter African cherry trees. Massive eagle ferns cover the ground, along with forest bitterberry and woody tangles of purple flowering mimulopsis. The diversity of edible plants and herbs in Bwindi satisfies even the largest forest residents: mountain gorillas.

It is mid December, and the dry season has begun. Overnight, the temperature dropped to 9 °C. A cool mist blanketed the mountainside during the early morning. By midday, the sun has warmed the forest to 27 °C. A mountain gorilla family relaxes in the shade, munching on fig leaves. Suddenly, one of the females sighs heavily. The other gorillas realise something exciting is about to happen. Soon they will have a new family member.

Scent signals

Gorillas produce body odours unique to the individual. These scents are used to identify each other in the dense forest. Smells also change to indicate emotions such as anger, fear or love.

CHAPTER ONE

LIFE BEGINS

Gorillas belong to the group of mammals called primates. These are animals with highly developed brains and gripping hands. Gorillas and their closest relatives – chimpanzees, orangutans and humans – are great apes. These primates have the largest brains. Monkeys and prosimians are also primates. They have tails, snouts and smaller brains. All apes and most other primates have five toes on each foot and four fingers and a thumb on each hand. This allows them to hold and control objects. Primates have fingernails and toenails instead of claws. Newborns have a weak grip. A primate mother must hold her newborn to her chest so it can feed on the milk she produces. Within a few weeks, it grows strong enough to hang on to its mother's hair by itself.

BWINDI MOUNTAIN GORILLA MILESTONES

DAY (1)

- Born
- Covered with sparse fur
- Weight: 2 kg
- Height: 25cm

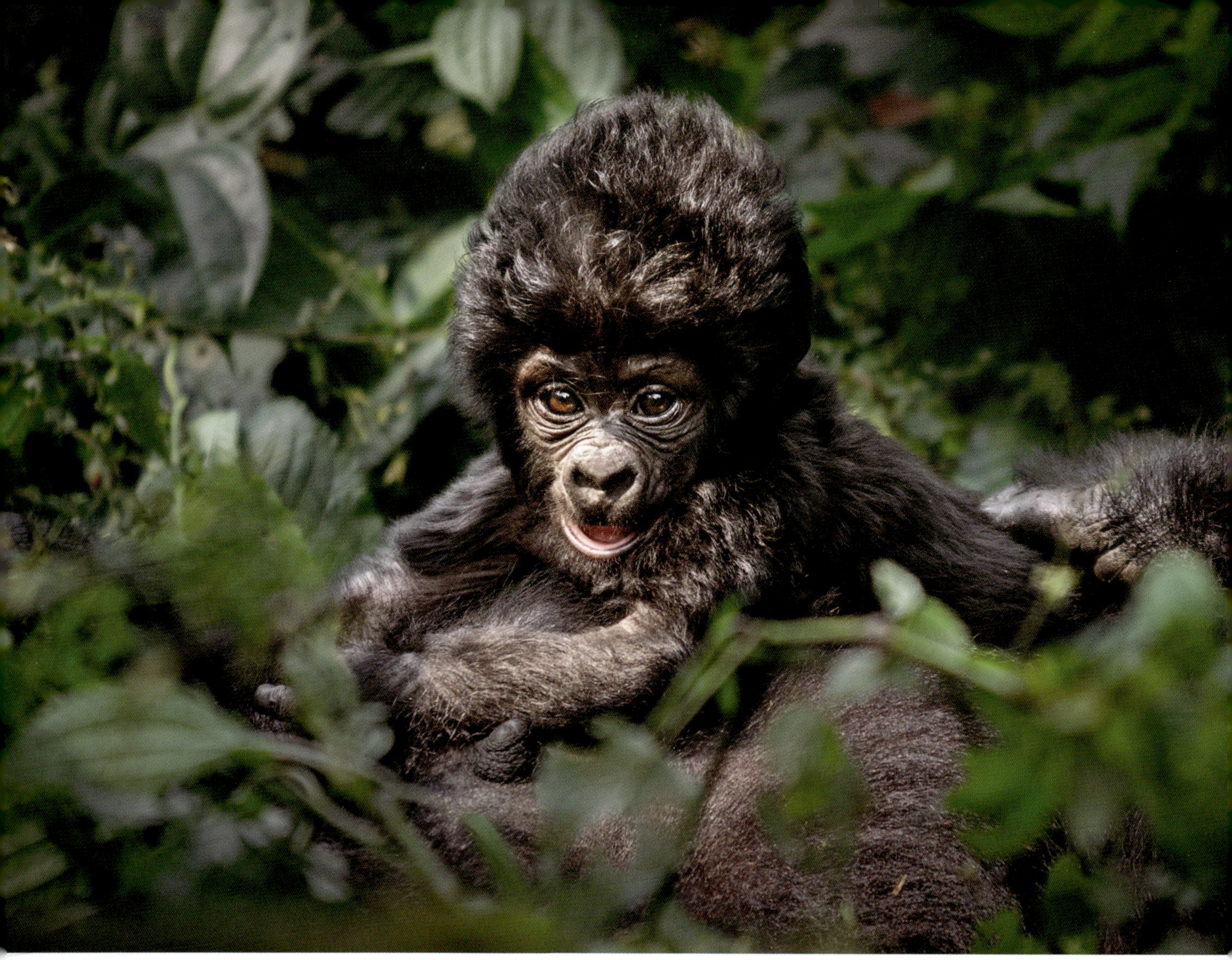

Welcome to the World

In Bwindi, the female mountain gorilla rolls onto her back and rubs her belly, which has been growing bigger for eight and a half months. She groans softly. After some effort, she gives birth to a tiny baby. She lifts him tenderly. The mother gorilla slurps fluid from her infant's mouth and nose, clearing his airway. As he takes his first deep breath, he inhales the scent of his mother. Soon, the newborn will learn to recognise scent signals, which indicate anger, distress or calmness.

There are two gorilla species – western and eastern. These are divided into four subspecies. The mountain gorilla is a subspecies of the eastern gorilla. Most gorillas have short black hair, but mountain gorillas have longer hair and thicker body fat suited to their mountainous habitat, where temperatures can drop below freezing. Male gorillas average 1.5–1.8 m in height and weigh up to 227 kg. Females average just under 1.5 m tall and weigh 70–91 kg. Newborns weigh about 2 kg and grow quickly.

Mature males between 8 and 11 years old are called blackbacks. Around age 12, white hair begins to grow on their backs from their shoulders to their rumps, and they become silverbacks. Gorillas live in troops, or family groups, of 5 to 30 members that are

CLOSE-UP
Sagittal crest

Male gorillas have a bony ridge across the top of their skulls. This is the sagittal crest. It adds power to the gorilla's jaws. A gorilla's bite is nearly eight times stronger than a human's.

(8) WEEKS

- ▸ Begins crawling on all fours
- ▸ Teeth have appeared

(10) WEEKS

- ▸ Begins eating fruit and leaves
- ▸ Weight: 6 kg
- ▸ Height: 32 cm

run by the strongest silverback. He protects the troop from predators, fathers babies and resolves conflicts among members. He may have to defend his position from rival silverbacks. Other mature males are ranked below the leading silverback. Females and their immature offspring are below the males, while females without offspring have the lowest status.

Diet

Gorillas eat seeds, leaves, stems, roots, fruits, flowers, bark and fungi. They also consume grubs and insects that are on these items. Gorillas eat up to 18 kg of vegetation each day.

First Meal

As the sun sets, the temperature starts to drop in the forest. The mother gorilla holds her infant close, covering his body with both hands to keep him warm. The infant's slender fingers curl around strands of her fur. He lets out a soft grunt as his tiny mouth finds milk. The milk provides everything the infant needs. Sugars and fats will strengthen his body, hormones will help him grow, and antibodies will give him the best chance of survival.

Gorillas live in troops of FIVE to THIRTY MEMBERS.

(3.5) MONTHS

- Begins riding on mother's back
- Regularly plays with other infants

Long limbs

Gorillas' arms are longer and stronger than their legs. Gorillas can stand and walk upright, but they usually walk using their hind feet and the knuckles of their hands.

CHAPTER TWO

EARLY ADVENTURES

During their first year of life, gorilla infants depend on their mothers for food and protection, but the whole troop participates in the nurturing of infants. Older females teach immature females how to babysit infants. To strengthen infants' muscles, adults gently wrestle with the babies and swing them by their arms and legs. When infants are about 10 weeks old, they start to play with one another. They also begin eating fruit and leaves. As they age, they wrestle and play-fight, chase each other up and down trees and roll down hills. Such activities strengthen young gorillas' bodies. They learn co-operation skills, too. Juveniles will continue to supplement their diets with their mothers' milk for up to four years. Gorillas digest food slowly. They spend most of the day

7 MONTHS

- Can easily jump off mother and climb back on
- Eating mostly solid foods
- Weight: 11 kg
- Height: 46 cm

9 MONTHS

- Takes first steps on hind legs
- Climbs trees with ease

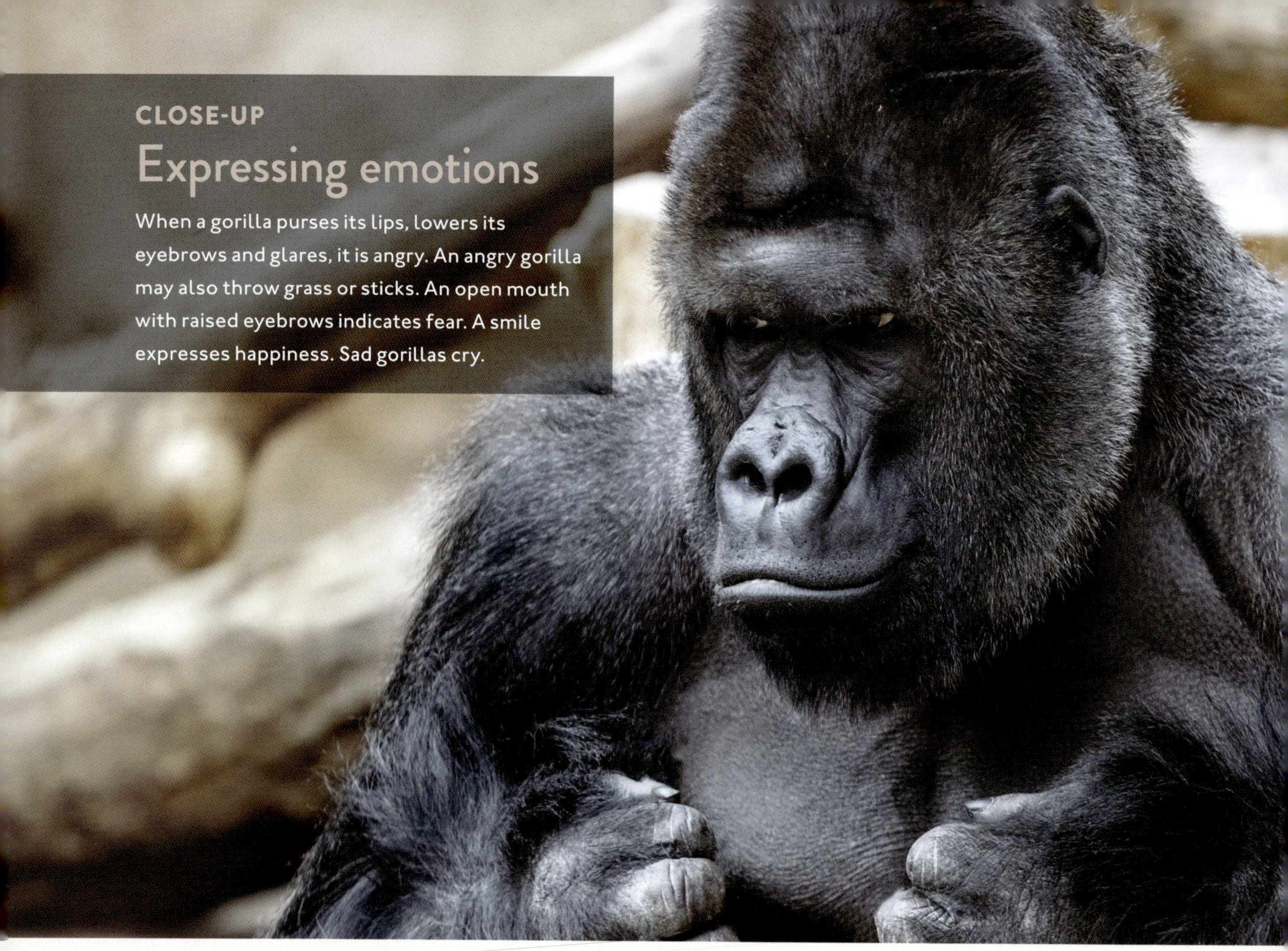

FEATURED FAMILY

Look Who's Crawling

The Bwindi gorilla infant is now two months old. He has worked out how to crawl. He sets off toward his father, who sits nearby, munching a stalk of bamboo. The infant approaches the massive silverback and reaches out with unsteady fingers. He touches the long, black hair covering the silverback's leg. With a snort, the silverback extends one finger and gently taps the infant on the top of his head. The infant squeals and loses his balance, tipping over and landing on his face in the grass. The silverback tenderly pats the infant's back. One day this tiny gorilla will be as big and powerful as his father.

When **INFANTS** are about **10 WEEKS** old, they start to **PLAY** with one another.

(3) **YEARS**

- No longer rides on mother's back
- Nests with other juveniles in trees
- Weight: 18 kg
- Height: 81 cm

foraging, eating and napping. A troop may travel about 800 m (half a mile) each day as it forages. While eating, gorillas sit cross-legged. They often gather and fold food into a kind of sandwich. They bite and shred food with their sharp teeth. Gorillas may eat only certain parts of a food source by tearing or scooping out what they want. They leave the leftovers in a neat pile. Gorillas rarely drink water. They get most of the moisture they need from their food or by licking dew off leaves. After a full day of activity, gorillas sleep 13 to 15 hours at night.

Teeth

Gorillas have 32 teeth. Sharp front teeth cut through bamboo, bark and other thick plant material. Strong back molars grind food to a pulp. Silverbacks have long, sharp canine teeth used mainly to threaten rivals.

——— FEATURED FAMILY ———

Give It a Try

In the Bwindi forest, the silverback climbs a tree and knocks a dozen overripe, red fruits to the ground. A juvenile scoops up a fruit and tears into it. The silverback climbs down and races to slap away the fruit. He has not yet given the youngster permission to eat. The infant gorilla watches the drama unfold. Then he sneaks over to the shattered fruit and snatches a tiny piece, shoving this first taste of fruit into his mouth before anyone notices.

(4) **YEARS**

- ▸ No longer drinks mother's milk
- ▸ Witnesses birth of younger sibling
- ▸ Weight: 19 kg
- ▸ Height: 94 cm

Calls

Silverbacks scream from close up or hoot from a distance to warn off enemies. Three quick barks ask, "Where are you?". A soft rumble tells others that there is food to share, but loud grunting means "I'm not sharing". Calm gorillas sing, "Mwaaah, hwah, hwah", and playful gorillas chuckle.

CHAPTER THREE

LIFE LESSONS

Young male gorillas learn to lead by watching their troop's silverback, whose commands are followed without hesitation. The lead silverback tells his troop when they should eat, rest, travel and sleep. During calm periods, he may rumble, grunt or snort softly to convey reassurance. Silence can also be an important form of communication. When the silverback falls silent and looks intently at his surroundings, he is telling his troop to be quiet and listen – something is out there, and it could be dangerous. When a sudden threat is perceived, he may emit a loud scream. This signal sends youngsters up trees and adults scattering to take cover.

While silverbacks protect their troops by threatening yet rarely fighting, young males still practise the chest-beating and biting skills

(8) YEARS

- Leaves mother's company
- Joins adolescent group
- Weight: 34 kg
- Height: 1.3 m

(12) YEARS

- Grey hairs appear on back
- Moves up in troop rank to just below head silverback

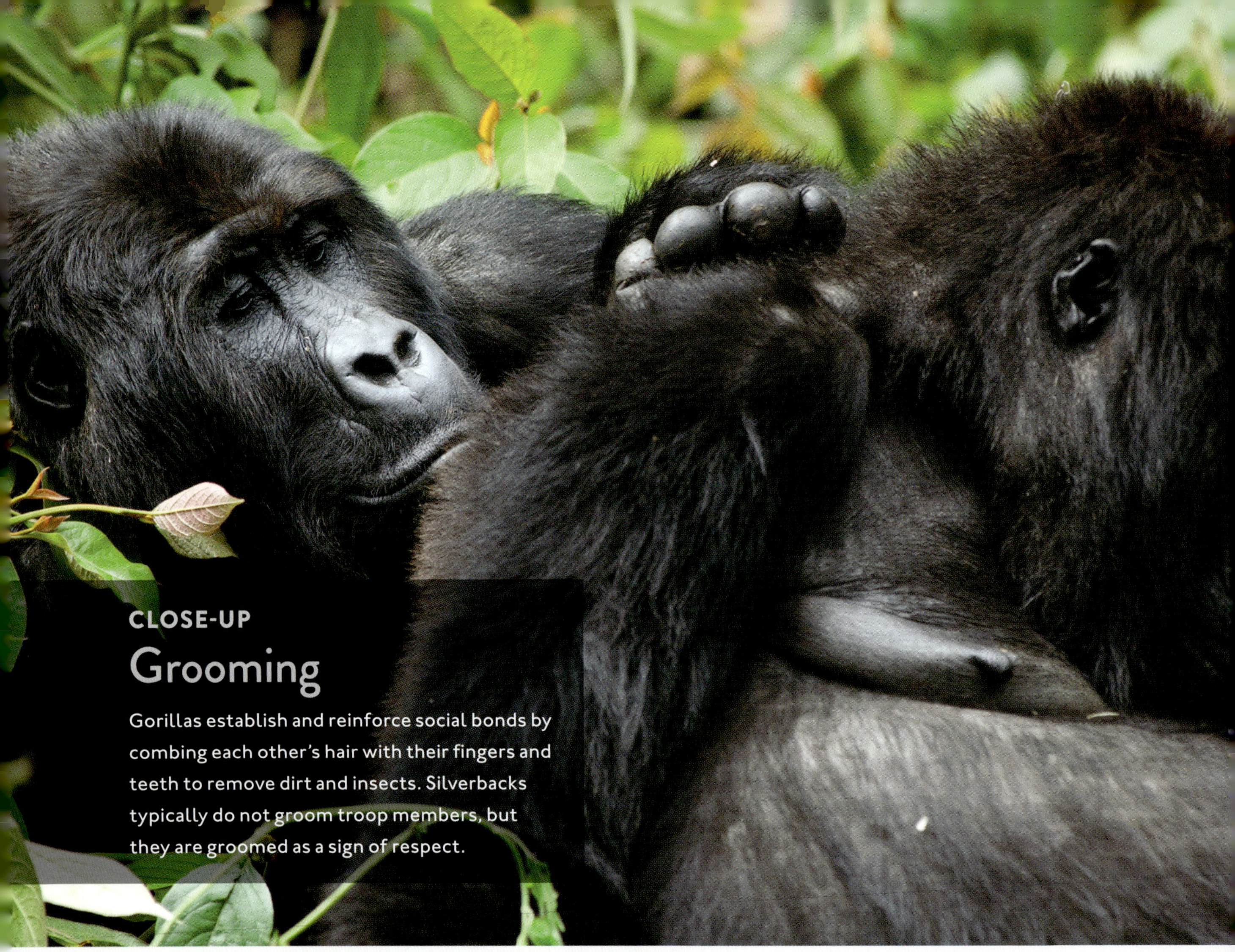

Grooming

Gorillas establish and reinforce social bonds by combing each other's hair with their fingers and teeth to remove dirt and insects. Silverbacks typically do not groom troop members, but they are groomed as a sign of respect.

This Is How It's Done

As night falls on the Bwindi forest, a leopard steps out of the underbrush. Its gaze lands on the young gorilla, now three years old, climbing a tree to make a nest. In an instant, the silverback jumps to his feet. The juvenile freezes, watching intently. The silverback tears up a handful of grass and throws it. He slaps his chest and angrily screams, "Waaaah!" The leopard disappears. Copying this display, the young gorilla slaps a palm against his own chest and squeals. Then he scurries up the tree.

that may prove necessary to lead their own troops. As the youngsters grow up, they play-fight and practise aggressive displays. They stand and beat their chests and throw sticks and mud. They may charge at each other and even tumble around, nipping arms and legs. When they are 10 to 13 years old, young silverbacks leave their family troops. They either take over an old silverback's troop or gather roaming females who have left their families. Gorillas will not mate with siblings or with unrelated gorillas they have grown up with, whom they consider stepsiblings.

Females also leave their troop when they mature. They begin mating around age 10, typically giving birth once every 4 to 6 years.

(13) **YEARS**

- ▸ Chased away from troop
  by head silverback
- ▸ Weight: 191 kg
- ▸ Height: 1.6 m

(15) **YEARS**

- ▸ Establishes new troop with two females
- ▸ Mates for the first time
- ▸ Weight: 218 kg
- ▸ Height: 1.7 m

Females breed only with the silverback leading their troop or his second-in-command (if the silverback allows it). A mother gorilla keeps her offspring close for the first two to three years, carrying the baby on her back as she travels and guarding it as it sleeps. Young females learn nurturing skills by serving as babysitters during the day and nesting with other adolescents in trees at night. Gorillas in **captivity** may live to be 50, but most wild gorillas live no more than 40 years.

Nests

Gorillas rarely sleep in the same place two nights in a row. Adults gather fresh piles of branches and leaves to make soft "mattresses" on the ground. For safety, juveniles make nests in trees.

— FEATURED FAMILY —

Practice Makes Perfect

The Bwindi gorilla is now four years old. His mother holds a new infant on her knee. The curious young gorilla comes closer to his baby sister. He extends a cautious finger toward the infant. She reaches out with a tiny hand and grasps her brother's finger. Though he spent the morning chasing and play-fighting with other adolescents in the troop, he is calm now. One day, when he is a huge silverback, he will have to be this gentle with his own fragile offspring.

25 YEARS

40 YEARS

▸ Troop has grown larger
▸ Father to 12 surviving offspring

▸ End of life

CHAPTER FOUR

GORILLA SPOTTING

Since the mid-20th century, gorilla populations have severely declined. The nations where gorillas live are poor, and many people are desperate for food. This leads to poaching, or illegal killing, of gorillas for **bushmeat**. Some gorillas have lost hands and feet in illegal snares that hunters set up to catch anything from rabbit-like hyraxes to African buffaloes. Baby gorillas are also captured for the illegal pet trade, which devastates gorilla troops. Another problem is **deforestation**. This displaces gorillas, contributing to the decline in their numbers.

Three African governments worked together to establish a refuge for mountain gorillas called the Virunga Conservation Area. It includes parts of Bwindi Impenetrable National Park in Uganda, Virunga National Park in the Democratic Republic of the Congo, and Volcanoes National Park in Rwanda. In 1978, primate researcher Dian Fossey founded the Digit Fund, which raised money to pay people to patrol mountain gorilla habitats and destroy traps. When Fossey was murdered in 1985 (probably by poachers), the fund was renamed the Dian Fossey Gorilla

Fund International in the United States and the Gorilla Organization in the United Kingdom. Thanks to people who have continued Fossey's work, the population of mountain gorillas has increased from about 300 to nearly 900 in recent decades. While this number is still very low, even modest growth is a good sign.

Cross River gorillas, a subspecies of the western gorilla, are not so fortunate. They are the world's most **endangered** great ape. Fewer than 300 mature individuals exist in an area of forest targeted for logging. Slightly smaller than their relatives, male Cross River gorillas average no more than 200 kg. They are extremely shy and difficult to study, which only increases their vulnerability. About 4,000 eastern lowland gorillas and roughly 100,000 western lowland gorillas live in the wild. Despite the higher numbers, these gorillas are also in trouble.

Gorillas share their world with people who struggle with civil war, disease and poverty. Park rangers tasked with protecting gorillas may be killed by poachers or forced to work with poachers in order to feed their families. Organisations around the world work with national and local governments in African countries to improve the protection of gorillas. They help develop better land-use plans to curb deforestation and provide education to local communities about the devastating effects of hunting gorillas. The continuation of such large-scale conservation efforts is vital to saving gorillas for future generations.

SNAPSHOTS

Koko was a **western lowland gorilla** who learned to communicate with humans using a version of American Sign Language.

Eastern lowland gorillas, also called Grauer's gorillas, are bigger than other gorilla subspecies, with males weighing up to 227 kg.

Western lowland gorillas inhabit lowland forests from Nigeria to Angola. Their range extends westward to the Central African Republic and parts of the Democratic Republic of the Congo.

The Digit Fund was named after Digit, Dian Fossey's favourite **mountain gorilla**. He was killed by poachers in 1977.

Michael, a **western lowland gorilla**, was Koko's companion. Koko taught him sign language, which he used to describe his experience with poachers.

Eastern lowland gorillas inhabit rainforests of the Democratic Republic of the Congo. They prefer flatter land than their mountain-dwelling cousins.

Cross River gorillas, named after their habitat on the Cameroon-Nigeria border, were discovered in 1904 but not closely studied until 1987.

Mountain gorillas are highly social, typically living in tight-knit troops of 6 to 12 members. Troops may grow to include up to 50 members, but this is rare.

Born in 1956 in Columbus Zoo, Ohio, USA, Colo was the first western lowland gorilla born in captivity. She lived for 60 years, making her the world's oldest known gorilla.

Cross River gorillas typically live in family groups of just four to seven individuals. But troops with as many as 18 members have been recorded.

A western lowland gorilla named Snowflake was the world's only known albino, or all-white, gorilla. He lived in Spain's Barcelona Zoo until his death in 2003.

The Democratic Republic of the Congo's Kahuzi-Biega National Park is home to the largest population (about 250) of protected eastern lowland gorillas.

Binti Jua is a western lowland gorilla at Brookfield Zoo in Illinois, USA. When a three-year-old boy fell into her enclosure in 1996, she carried him to safety.

WORDS to Know

antibodies   substances that destroy other disease-carrying substances

bushmeat   the meat of wild animals killed for food in tropical parts of the world

captivity   living in a place from which escape is not possible

deforestation   the clearing or thinning of forests by humans

endangered   at risk of dying out completely

hormones   chemical substances produced in the body that control the activity of certain cells and organs

juveniles   young animals that have not yet reached full adulthood

mammals   animals that have a backbone and hair or fur, give birth to live young, and produce milk to feed their young

species   a group of living beings with shared characteristics and the ability to reproduce with one another

LEARN MORE

Books

Daly, Ruth. *Bringing Back the Mountain Gorilla*. Crabtree, 2019.

Nichols, Michael. *Face to Face with Gorillas*. National Geographic Readers, 2019.

Redmond, Ian. *The Primate Family Tree*. Firefly Books, 2019.

Websites

"About Gorillas." The Gorilla Organisation. https://www.gorillas.org/about-gorillas/

"Gorilla Facts for Kids." Kiddle. https://kids.kiddle.co/Gorilla

"What Do Gorillas Eat? And Other Gorilla Facts." World Wildlife Fund. https://www.worldwildlife.org/stories/what-do-gorillas-eat-and-other-gorilla-facts

Documentaries

Nikwigiza, Novella and Rosenberg, Lucas. *Saving Gorillas: Giving Nature a Voice*. Aga Khan University Graduate School of Media and Communications, 2017.

Tassier, Lydia. *In the Land of the Gorillas*. Owendo Productions, 2015.

Taylor, Jonathan. *Koko: The Gorilla Who Talks to People*. BBC, 2016.

Note: Every effort has been made to ensure that any websites listed above were active at the time of publication. However, because of the nature of the Internet, it is impossible to guarantee that these sites will remain active indefinitely or that their contents will not be altered.

Visit

BLACKPOOL ZOO

*Home to six western lowland gorillas
who live on Gorilla Mountain.*

East Park Drive

Blackpool, Lancashire

FY3 8PP

BRISTOL ZOO

*Get close to a family of western lowland
gorillas at Gorilla Island.*

Bristol Zoo Gardens

Guthrie Road, Clifton, Bristol

BS8 3HA

HOWLETTS WILD ANIMAL PARK

*The largest group of gorillas in a British
wildlife park, run by a charity.*

Bekesbourne Lane

Littlebourne, Kent

CT4 5EL

ZSL LONDON ZOO

*Experience the African rainforest in the
heart of London at Gorilla Kingdom.*

Regent's Park

London

NW1 4RY

INDEX